THE
HAUNTED GARDEN

DEATH AND
TRANSFIGURATION IN THE
FOLKLORE OF PLANTS

SHERYL HUMPHREY

The Haunted Garden: Death and Transfiguration in the Folklore of Plants

ISBN 978-1-300-55364-9

This book is made possible (in part) by a DCA Art Fund Grant from the Council on the Arts & Humanities for Staten Island, with public funding from the New York City Department of Cultural Affairs.

DEDICATION

For Edward Coppola, who walks beside me in our own beautiful haunted garden.

For my sister, Elizabeth Scarpino, who shares my love of the subject and who provided helpful and discerning suggestions.

For my mother, Mitzi Humphrey, for always believing in me.

Now I shall tell of things that change, new being out of old....

Ovid, *The Metamorphoses,* Invocation
[Horace Gregory translation]

CONTENTS

INTRODUCTION

It is for a reason that monuments and memorials to the dead often include a garden or plantings, and that cemeteries are as lushly landscaped as the finest pleasure gardens. Gardens are traditionally places of respite and peace, where one can find a pleasant solitude suitable for reflection.

But it is also in the garden that we observe constant reminders that death follows life follows death in endless cycles. The joyful springtime exuberance of new growth, the summer glory of the flowers, and the abundant autumn harvest have always been celebrated. But beyond the happy, sunny floral display lies a different landscape: the dark garden. In this haunted garden the foliage rustles like whispers, the dense evergreens stand like sentinels, the decaying leaves smell of sweet rot, and the lichen-covered statuary appears strange and startling. There is an undeniable feel of the uncanny as a cloud obscures the sunlight and the warm breeze becomes a chill.

In my readings in mythology, folklore, and gardening I have come across myriad references to plants associated with tales of death, ghosts, and people transforming into flowers or trees. These tales are not about deaths caused by poisonous plants. Rather, they are strange stories and legends in which plants are intertwined with a human's passage to another state of being.

Metamorphosis is observed regularly in Nature, whether it be a seed sprouting first leaves or a butterfly emerging from a caterpillar's chrysalis. Through close contact with Nature in the cultivated garden or farm, a profound sense of the relationship of human to plant can develop, indeed a sense of the interconnectedness of all things. Perhaps the botanical stories of human death and transfiguration that came down through the ages were first inspired by early humans' reverence and respect for, and dependence upon, plants as food, shelter, and fuel. Or perhaps these striking tales developed from the realization that a landscape's beauty is born out of the death of the beauties before it:

Behold this compost! behold it well!

Perhaps every mite has once formed part of a sick person— Yet behold!

The grass covers the prairies,

The bean bursts noiselessly through the mould in the garden,

The delicate spear of the onion pierces upward,

The apple-buds cluster together on the apple branches,

The resurrection of the wheat appears with pale visage out of its grave....

— from "This Compost" by Walt Whitman

These ancient themes of metamorphosis and the dark garden seem to be deeply embedded in human consciousness. References to botanical myths and legends still abound even today. Contemporary explorations of plant/person transfiguration can be found in all forms of art and pop culture.

This little book is hardly comprehensive on the subject; it is intended as a choice sampler of, and introduction to, a rather specific and arcane aspect of botanical lore. The legends range in tone from the tragic to the humorous, from the silly to the psychologically insightful, but all of them are weird. I would like to share some of these peculiar, fascinating bits of plant folklore that I have been collecting from obscure books for many years. Readers may find, as I have, that these strange old stories add a pleasant frisson to their enjoyment of the garden.

CHAPTER ONE

GODS, GODDESSES, AND MORTALS

Any discussion of the theme of humans changing into non-human forms must acknowledge the importance and influence of Ovid's *Metamorphoses* in Western culture. The long narrative poem in Latin, completed by the Roman poet in the year 8 A.D., ambitiously attempted to link all the ancient Greek myths to the Roman myths of Ovid's day in a hybrid of world history, mock-epic, and episodic storytelling.

Many of the myths and stories in *Metamorphoses* focus on interactions of gods and goddesses, sometimes with mortals. These interactions often result in characters' bodies being transformed into animals, stones, stars, streams, or (of interest here) into flowers, trees, and other plants.

9

The vivid, psychologically probing tales in Ovid's poem were immensely popular in his own time and through the Middle Ages. His startling themes and characters inspired generations of poets, playwrights, artists, composers, and choreographers, and the influence continues today.

Below are some of the most celebrated botanical transfigurations described in *Metamorphoses*. Additional human/plant myths from Ovid appear in this book's later chapters as well.

In Ovid's version of the Greek myth, Apollo (or Phoebus), the great god of light and the sun, mocked Eros (or Cupid) for playing at being an archer. Eros took revenge by choosing two special arrows from his quiver: one that incited love, and one that induced hatred. He shot Apollo with the love arrow and the beautiful nymph Daphne with the arrow of hate. Apollo was now inflamed with love for the maiden, but she abhorred him.

Overcome with obsessive desire, Apollo relentlessly pursued the nymph in a quest to make her his own, while Daphne, overcome with revulsion at the thought of his embrace, fled from his grasping arms. Eventually he was about to overtake her. Resisting Apollo until the last, Daphne called upon her father the river god to help her, by marring her beauty that she thought had brought the calamity upon her. In answer to her prayer, she was suddenly changed: her feet rooted in the ground; her skin became bark; her arms transformed into branches: she was a bay laurel tree (*Laurus nobilis*).

Apollo's arms held in her vain, for Daphne was now transfigured. But Eros's arrow still kept his love alive. The bay laurel became sacred to the god. He wore a crown of her leaves, and "to wear the laurels" would thereafter be an honor. The tree would be evergreen – immortal, in a sense – as a testament to his devotion.

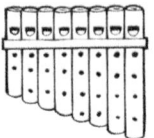

The Greek god Pan, known for his numerous amorous adventures, desired a water-nymph named Syrinx. She was a devoted follower of the goddess Artemis, and like the goddess defended her chastity. She fled from the goat-god's advances, and he chased her through the woodlands of Arcadia until they reached the River Ladon. In desperation and fearing her fate at the hands of Pan, Syrinx cried out to her sister water-nymphs of the river to help her. Just as Pan was wrapping his arms around her to catch her, he found himself grasping an armful of reeds. Syrinx had been transfigured into the slender, graceful reeds of the water's edge.

As the winds blew softly along the riverbank, Pan heard a beautiful, haunting sound. He cut some of the reeds and used them to fashion his pipes, which he called Syrinx in honor of the virtuous, beautiful nymph. Pan-pipes or Pan flutes are musical instruments still played today.

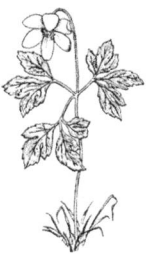

The handsome youth Adonis, a mortal god of beauty and desire, was beloved by Venus (Aphrodite). He was attacked by a wild boar while hunting, and collapsed on the forest floor as his lifeblood ran in rivulets from his wounds. When she heard his cries of pain, Venus rushed to him, but he died.

Remembering that the goddess Persephone had been able to change a nymph into a mint plant, Venus declared that she would honor Adonis by transforming his blood into a flower that would spring up annually in testament to her mourning. She sprinkled the spilled blood with fragrant nectar, and from it was created the bright-red anemone. Thereafter, every year, anemone flowers appeared in flowing red masses like the slain Adonis's blood. The beautiful anemone, like Adonis, is short-lived. Its name derives from the Greek for "daughter of the wind," and sadly the flower's vibrant petals are scattered by the wind soon after a brief period of bloom.

Ovid mentions Crocus and Smilax in passing as having been turned into flowers. The pair are yet another example of tangled, contradictory references in mythology. One of the most-mentioned versions of their story says that Crocus (or Krokos) was a handsome mortal youth who loved the woodland nymph Smilax. The nymph was flattered by his amorous attentions and briefly flirted with him, then rejected him. Crocus wasted away for love of her, and became transformed into a little purple flower, the saffron crocus (*Crocus sativus*). Simultaneously, Smilax was transformed into a vining greenbriar.

Ovid's version of the myth of Narcissus pairs the handsome young man with the talkative mountain nymph Echo. Echo fell in love with Narcissus but he rejected her. Shunned, Echo slowly wasted away until all that was left of her was a voice. The uncaring Narcissus then stopped to rest by a quiet spring where he noticed his reflection in the still waters of the pool. Captivated by his own beautiful image, he fell in love with himself. Of course, the love remained unrequited; if he reached out to embrace his lover, the lover disappeared and Narcissus's arms were plunged into the cold water. He could never have what he wanted, and like Echo, he gradually wasted away, and died. In the place of his body was a narcissus flower. The pale, delicate flowers sometimes still nod their heads downward, as if admiring their own reflection in a woodland pool.-

The myth of Myrrha has many versions, the best known probably being the one found in Ovid's *Metamorphoses*. The tale is strange and deeply disturbing – a story of an obsessed young woman, incest, transfiguration, the birth of a god, and a musing on the taboos that serve as demarcations between nature and civilization. Myrrha, who could have had her pick of princes, fell in love with her father Cinyras and tricked him into sexual intercourse by posing as another woman. When Cinyras discovered her true identity, he raised his sword at her, but Myrrha fled. For nine months she was on the run – and pregnant. Fearing both the condemnation of living and the damnation of dying, she prayed to the gods: "Make me a thing that neither lives nor dies." She was immediately transformed into a fragrant myrrh tree, her human tears turning into myrrh resin. Still pregnant even though she was now a tree, Myrrha, attended by dryads, gave birth to a boy, Adonis.

Three legends of classical Greece, though not from Ovid's *Metamorphoses*, tell of an angry or jealous goddess turning a nymph into a myrtle (*Myrtus communis*), an evergreen, fragrant small tree or bush. In one tale, the nymph Myrsine or Myréne wins a running race against the goddess Pallas Athena. In a flash of anger, Pallas kills her. From the nymph's body grows a myrtle, which the remorseful goddess treasures forever after.

In a second legend, Myréne is a priestess of Venus. Myréne falls in love with a young man and intends to marry him. But a priestess of Venus is not allowed to marry, and the offended goddess punishes her by changing her into a myrtle tree. A third version of the myth is similar, with the difference that even though Venus turns Myréne into a myrtle, she shows her affection for the nymph by ordaining that the tree associated with her would be always green and lovely, and with a pleasing fragrance.

BEYOND OVID'S IMMORTALS

The Bhagavata tells of two sons of Kuwera, the God of Riches, who were changed into a pair of Arjuna trees (*Terminalia arjuna*). The young brothers Manigriva and Nalakuvera were victims of a curse cast by the holy sage Narada as punishment for their disrespectful drunken behavior. In Hindu legend the two enormous, enchanted trees stood in the courtyard of Krishna's mother. One day little Krishna wedged a wooden mortar between the trees, causing them to become uprooted. With the spell broken, the brothers were released from the trees, and became devoted followers of Lord Krishna.

An ancient Chinese legend (likely Taoist) describes how Yaoji, a daughter of Yandi, died at a young age before she could be married. Rebelling against having to descend to the underworld, she became transformed into a tree. Later, a stone marked the spot where she was worshiped. From her permanent place on Mount Wushan she surveyed the vista of peaks and gorges. When it rained on the mountain, it was said that Yaoji was weeping with regret for her lost life.

When the Cherokee were first living on the earth, they thought that it would be better if there was no night. They asked the Creator to take away the night. The Creator granted their prayer and so there was only day. But after a while the people realized that a constant day only meant that it was always too hot, the weeds grew too thickly among the corn and squash, and the forest was almost impenetrable with overgrowth.

They admitted their mistake and beseeched the Creator to take away the day and have only night. The Creator was puzzled, since things were mostly created in pairs of opposites. But out of love for the people the Creator gave them what they requested.

Soon enough, the people discovered that a constant night was an even worse idea.

With no sunlight, all the crops stopped growing, and the people could not see to hunt for game. The world was very cold, and it was impossible to gather enough firewood in the endless darkness. Death came to many of the people.

The surviving people gathered again to humble themselves before the Creator. They asked for forgiveness for not appreciating the perfect and balanced world of day and night that the Creator had made for them. They wanted to go back to the way it was before.

Yet again, the Creator honored their request. He restored the balance of night and day to the world, which brought back better weather, plentiful crops, and good health to the people so that they could hunt for game and gather firewood. The people were grateful for their lives, were good to one another, and were happy. The Creator was pleased, but also sorry that so many people had died during the period of endless night. For this reason, the Created gathered the spirits of the dead people and put them in a new kind of tree, a red cedar (*Juniperus virginiana*). And today, if you are Tsalagi (Cherokee) and you see a handsome red cedar, or smell its fragrant wood, or hear it resonating from a traditional tribal drum, remember to honor the tree as your ancestor.

CHAPTER TWO

THE DOOMED LOVERS

As may be seen in the previous chapter, in much of the botanical folklore involving death and transfiguration, unrequited love plays an important role, as does rejected love. But mutual love also figures in plant legends. Here are some of the stories and myths that feature pairs of lovers whose spirits now dwell in the Haunted Garden.

A story from Giovanni Boccaccio's Decameron (ca. 1350-53) was later adapted into a narrative poem by John Keats, *Isabella, or the Pot of Basil* (1818). The poem was the subject of paintings by Pre-Raphaelite artists William Holman Hunt and John Everett Millais. The tale involves a fair young maiden Lisabetta (or Isabella) and her three brothers, wealthy merchants of Messina.

The brothers expected Isabella to marry a man suited to her high station in society, but she fell in love with handsome Lorenzo, who worked for the brothers. When the brothers discovered the relationship, they led Lorenzo to a remote place where they murdered and buried him. They told everyone, including Isabella, that they had sent Lorenzo abroad on business for them, and that he would not return for a long time.

The lovesick Isabella became more and more despairing as time passed with no word from Lorenzo. She feared that something evil had happened to him, but she knew not what. Each night she cried and called out Lorenzo's name, beseeching him to return to her. One night, his ghost appeared to her and told her the truth of how and where he was slain by her brothers.

In the morning, Isabella slipped away from the house with a trusted servant and went to the scene of the crime. Under the dead leaves, she noticed an area where the ground was soft, and began to dig. There lay the corpse of her lover, unblemished by decay. Unable to transport the body, and frantic from fear of her brothers, Isabella cut off the head from the body and took it home, where she lamented over Lorenzo's death and kissed his head a thousand times. To keep him with her, yet unseen by others, she buried the head in a large garden pot that she then planted with sweet basil.

Every day Isabella sat by the pot of basil, gazing and sighing at it longingly. Every day her grief overwhelmed her, and she wept so much that the basil was watered by her tears. The plants flourished from her attention, but she became weaker and weaker. Her brothers eventually discovered the source of her obsession, and secretly took away the pot and buried the head. With her health and spirit broken, Isabella piteously and continuously asked for the pot of basil, until she died from grief.

A common motif in several traditional English and Scottish popular ballads such as "Barbara Allen," "Lord Lovel," and "Lady Margret" is that of two intertwined plants springing from the graves of a tragic pair of dead lovers. These melancholy folk songs usually have a few verses with lyrics that describe two separate plants or trees joining together over adjoining burial spots. The interlaced branches and trunks symbolize the everlasting love between the couple and the uniting of their eternal souls.

In one of the many versions of "Barbara Allen," the last two stanzas illustrate this theme:

Barbara Allen was buried in the olde church yard,
Sweet William buried beside her.
Out of Sweet William's heart grew a red, red rose,
Out of Barbry Allen's, a briar.

They grew and grew in the olde church yard,
Till they could grow no higher.
At the end they formed a true lovers' knot,
And the Rose grew 'round the Briar.

A briar, noted for its thorns, is appropriate for Barbara Allen in this version, because earlier in the song it is implied that she is hard-hearted for having originally ignored William in his lovesick distress. Only after he dies – from want of her – does she decide she loves him, and then she herself dies of a broken heart. And from their graves, "the Rose grew 'round the Briar."

In Greek mythology, Princess Phyllis of Thrace fell in love with Demophoon, son of Theseus. They were to be married as soon as Demophoon returned from sailing home to Attica to put his affairs in order. He promised Phyllis that they would be reunited within an agreed-upon time. As the days and weeks passed, the lovesick Phyllis would watch from the shore, scanning the horizon for any sign of her betrothed, but to no avail.

The deadline for Demophoon's return passed, and Phyllis despaired of ever seeing him again. Believing that he had abandoned her or had perished, she grew so weak that she died of grief. (In another version of the tale, she hung herself from an almond tree.) In any case, the gods, having admired her for showing such faithfulness to her lover, took pity and did not allow her body to be buried, but instead transformed her into a living almond tree. Like Phyllis the devoted woman, the tree also gazed longingly at the sea, its limbs reaching out from the shore.

When Demophoon finally did sail back to Thrace, he was told of the events that had transpired in his absence. Stricken with grief and remorse, he threw himself at the tree, embracing its trunk and watering its roots with his tears. Touched by his display of love, the almond tree burst into lovely and fragrant bloom.

Not all the tales of couples buried side-by-side are about passion's sudden tragic end when the lovers are still young, beautiful, and in the prime of life. Ovid's story of the arboreal transformation of Baucis and Philemon celebrates the everlasting love shared by an old and long-married couple.

One day the gods Jupiter (Zeus or Jove) and Mercury (Hermes) decided to disguise themselves as mortals and visit the town of Phrygia. They were curious about how they would be received by the townspeople. Dressed as ordinary peasants, they would knock on the doors of the village houses requesting the then-common courtesy of hospitality for strangers or travelers. They stopped at a thousand homes but at every home they were rudely turned away.

Finally they reached a small thatched cottage, the home of Baucis and Philemon. The elderly married couple gladly and graciously welcomed the visitors inside their poor but cheerful home, and began preparing a supper of the best that they had to offer. (Ovid writes a delightful description of the rustic feast. He gently pokes fun at the simple foods served; Romans of his time valued complicated, exotic dishes. But the fresh, homestyle food would be quite appreciated by today's epicures.)

Baucis bustled about, building up the fire under the copper pot and laying out a spread of cherries, figs, nuts, olives, apples, and honeycomb from the cottage garden. Her husband Philemon took down a side of bacon from the rafters and sliced it to go with the baked eggs and cheese. Sweet wine was poured freely.

When the couple noticed that the wine bowl never emptied, they realized that something supernatural was happening, and that their guests were gods in disguise. They feared the gods' wrath at being served such humble fare. But the gods told Baucis and Philemon that they were the only people in the town who had treated the visitors decently. The gods would destroy the town, but their hosts would be spared.

The couple left town and hobbled up a mountain as directed. From there they watched a terrible flood cover everything except their little cottage. But now their cottage had become a shining marble temple. Mercury asked them what they wanted as a reward for their hospitality. The husband and wife asked to serve the gods in that temple, and to die together when their time came.

For many years they took care of the temple, as faithful servants to the gods. Then one day they felt that it was finally time to go. They embraced each other and said their goodbyes. They began to be transformed into trees, and became a linden and an oak. As the two trees grew together, their branches became so closely entwined that they seemed to grow from a single trunk. The venerable trees were a wonder to see, long after the temple had fallen to ruins. So lifelike was their tender companionship – like a loving couple helping each other in old age.

Today the growth process from which such a curious specimen develops is known as inosculation. Such conjoined trees are often nicknamed "husband and wife trees" or "marriage trees."

CHAPTER THREE

FUNERALS, GRAVES, AND CEMETERIES

Honoring the dead with flowers is a custom that dates back to earliest recorded history. The varieties and placement of flowers differed depending on location and historical period. Generally, cut flowers and floral wreaths were laid on coffins and graves. Sweetly fragrant flowers and herbs were used to mask the odor of decomposition. Flowers, flowering shrubs, and trees were planted around tombs and graves to enhance the peacefulness of the deceased's repose, and to beautify and freshen the surrounding ground.

Roses and white lilies were choice flowers for the dead, as were everlasting flowers such as amaranth. In the Americas, marigolds and carnations were customary. Evergreens such as cedar, cypress, yew, and pine, whose needles retain their color year-round even when deciduous trees are bare, were symbols of everlasting life and were planted liberally in cemeteries.

Today's "green burial" movement includes eco-friendly coffins that resemble large woven baskets, made of sustainable native willows. Willow trees have a long association with death, the underworld, and grief, but also with immortality. The mythological poet Orpheus carried willow branches for protection when he journeyed to the underworld. The ancient Druids supposedly burned their sacrificial victims in woven baskets. Weeping willows (*Salix babylonica*) were native to China, and became very popular cemetery plantings when brought to the West. Their picturesque "weeping" habit signified mourning and sadness. A coppiced or pollarded willow – cut back severely to encourage new growth of the long branches good for weaving – is a symbol of renewal and rebirth. It was a custom to plant a willow tree as a kind of surrogate for one's self, so that one's life would continue through the vital tree after one's death.

In Shakespeare's *Hamlet*, Laertes says at his sister Ophelia's burial: "Lay her i' the earth; / And from her fair and unpolluted flesh / May violets spring!" Sweet violets (*Viola odorata*) have a long association with death and funerals, but also with immortality and resurrection. They were placed in graves for remembrance, and scattered in tombs to banish foul or poisonous vapors. In Greek mythology, Persephone was gathering violets and lilies when she was abducted by Hades and taken to the Underworld.

Violets were also an essential part of the ancient Greco-Roman spring festival of Cybele and Attis. A pine tree would be cut and placed in the temple, then wreathed in violets, symbolic of the strange and violent death and rebirth of Attis, a mortal who became a god of vegetation. In one legend, he castrated himself under a pine tree, and as he bled to death, violets sprang up from his blood. At the festival, novice priests of Cybele (the goddess who loved Attis) would ritually re-create the scene and emasculate themselves in sacrifice.

The folk tale of Cinderella has many variants around the world. The first published version (1697) by Charles Perrault is the basis of the 1950 Walt Disney animated film. Cinderella's dead mother is not mentioned; we know only that the young girl's father has a second wife. When Cinderella's wicked stepmother and cruel stepsisters try to keep her hidden from the bride-seeking Prince, it is her fairy godmother who magically provides her with a beautiful gown, glass slippers, and transportation to the royal ball that changes her destiny.

But in "Aschenputtel [or Ash Maiden]," the 1812 Brothers Grimm version of the Cinderella fairy tale, there is no fairy godmother. This darker tale begins with the death of Cinderella's mother. The woman is buried in the garden, and her loving young daughter visits the grave daily. Cinderella's father remarries, and as in the Perrault version, Cinderella is treated cruelly by her stepmother and stepsisters.

The stepsisters ask the father to bring them expensive clothes and jewels from his travels, but Cinderella requests only "the first twig, dear Father, that brushes against your hat when you turn your face to come homewards." Her father saves her a hazel twig from a green copse he passes through. Cinderella plants the cutting on her mother's grave and cries so much over it that the twig rapidly grows into a thriving hazel tree.

The tree on her mother's grave is where Cinderella pours out her grief and despair over her troubles. Soon a little bird nests in the tree and consoles her and talks to her about her problems, clearly channeling the spirit of the mother. The bird also is able to grant wishes, and produces the elegant clothes Cinderella needs to attend the grand ball. In the end Cinderella and her Prince are happily wed, but only after the stepsisters are gruesomely eliminated from the competition.

The Grimms' eerie version of Cinderella lives on in contemporary culture. Most notably, it figures in the Stephen Sondheim and James Lapine musical, *Into the Woods*, and its song "Cinderella at the Grave." In the play's staging, the character of Cinderella's mother communicates with her daughter directly from within the tree, instead of through a bird intermediary.

In India, Tulsi (*Ocimum sanctum* or *Ocimum tenuiflorum*) is known as holy basil. (It is a different plant than the basil of Italian cuisine, *Ocimum basilicum*.) This holy herb is dedicated to the Hindu god Vishnu. Holy basil is considered to be an incarnation of the goddess Tulsi, sometimes known as a wife of Vishnu. In Hindu mythology, Tulsi had been a mortal woman

41

of great piety and devotion to Vishnu. When she sacrificed herself on her mortal husband's funeral pyre, her soul was transferred to the green herb.

Another Hindu legend of India holds that holy basil is actually Lakshmi, Vishnu's beloved chief consort, in disguise. In sympathy with Lakshmi, the god feels pain if the plant is hurt or damaged, and he refuses to hear the prayers of anyone who mistreats it. However, Vishnu's followers wear rosaries fashioned from the seeds of the holy basil, and they use the leaves for sacred rituals. A leaf placed on the body at death helps ensure that the soul is welcomed into heaven.

Holy basil was also associated with death in Egypt, where its flowers were strewn by women over the final resting places of their loved ones, and in Iran and Malaysia, where it was planted on graves.

The Greek sculptor and architect Callimachus (active later half of 5th century B.C.) is credited with having invented the Corinthian style of capital, one of the classical orders of architecture. A Corinthian capital is ornate and includes two rows of ornamental carvings of acanthus leaves. The large, spiny leaves of the acanthus plant curl over into sculptural curves that inspired the Corinthian aesthetic. *Acanthus mollis* and *Acanthus spinosus*, both found throughout the Mediterranean region, are the species probably referenced in the carvings.

The Roman writer Vitruvius, in his celebrated treatise *On Architecture* (ca. 15 B.C.), relates the story of how Callimachus chanced upon the acanthus motif. A little girl had died, and her nurse had gathered a few of the child's toys in a votive basket and placed it on the grave. Eventually an acanthus plant grew up through and around the woven basket. Callimachus noticed it one day, and was intrigued by the decorative quality of the natural arrangement of the leaves.

CHAPTER FOUR

CHRISTIAN ICONOGRAPHY

The crucifixion of Jesus Christ is the basis of a large subcategory of the subject of death and transfiguration in plant folklore, legends that arose outside of the actual New Testament biblical scripture. Various trees are said to have been chosen to provide the wood to make the cross on which Jesus died. Several different plants are supposedly the source of the crown of thorns, acacia for example. Many kinds of flowers were believed to have sprung up from Christ's drops of blood upon the ground, or to have acquired their color from the sacred blood. In one legend, blackberry bramble runners

45

were used to fashion the crown of thorns, and the blackberries were stained dark from the spilled blood.

Two flowers in particular embody the story of the crucifixion of Jesus. Generations of children in the southern United States (this author included) grew up learning the tale of the flowering dogwood tree (*Cornus florida*). As the legend goes, in Jesus's time, the dogwood was then a towering tree prized for its strength. Its wood was said to have been selected to construct the cross that was used to kill Christ's body. But the dogwood tree was horrified at having been used for this terrible purpose. Jesus, compassionate even in his suffering, assured the tree that it would never have to be used for a cross again. Instead, it would grow only as a small, slender tree that branches at the trunk.

But in celebration of the Resurrection, every spring around Easter the dogwood tree blooms, and within the flowers lies even more symbolism. The four lovely white "petals" (actually bracts) approximate the shape of a cross. The outer tip of each bract is deeply notched and stained a rusty red, in remembrance of how Christ's hands and feet bled from the wounds of being nailed to the cross. The circle of green flower-heads in the center represents the crown of the thorns.

Similarly, the passion flower or passion vine (*Passiflora*) was seen by colonial Spanish Christian missionaries in the Americas in the 15th and 16th centuries as embodying the Passion theology. To the missionaries' eyes, this distinctively structured flower exhibited even more Christian symbols than the dogwood, and could be used to teach their religion to the unconverted.

The sharply pointed leaves represented the lance that pierced Jesus's side. The plant's tendrils represented the lash of the whips used in the flagellation of Christ by the Romans. Ten petals and ten sepals stood for those Apostles who were loyal to Christ (leaving out St. Peter, who denied Jesus, and of course Judas Iscariot). The shape of the ovary was compared to a chalice, or the Holy Grail; the filaments were like the crown of thorns; the stigmas stood for nails; and the anthers recalled the wounds of the lance and nails. The flower's blue and white colors, the same as the robe worn by the Virgin Mary, symbolized heaven and purity.

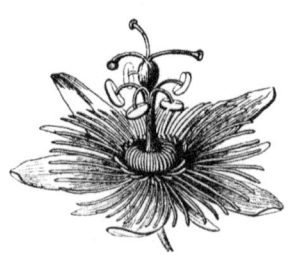

The redbud tree also has a Christian legend. Judas Iscariot, who betrayed Jesus for thirty pieces of silver and then hung himself out of shame and guilt, was said to have used a redbud tree for the hanging. The redbud trees wanted to make sure that they would never be used that way again, so they asked God to change them. The Lord granted their request, and from then on all redbud trees do not grow very tall, their branches are thin, and the limbs bow low to the ground, so that they cannot be used for hangings. In the spring the crimson buds cover the branches like streams of blood in remembrance of Christ's sacrifice, and the heart-shaped leaves symbolize God's love.

Mary, the Blessed Mother of Jesus, also figures in plant legends associated with transfiguration. The rose is one flower dedicated to her. A story from one of the medieval miracle collections tells how the monk Josbert loved to sing the Marian psalms every day. With great devotion he would repeat these five psalms that began with the letters of the name Maria. When he died, five roses miraculously appeared in his eyes, ears, and mouth.

The Madonna lily (Lilium candidum) is associated with the Virgin Mary, probably because its white color and graceful form symbolize the purity and love of the Blessed Mother. In one legend, the apostle Thomas received word that Mary had died. Thomas was known for his skepticism, having questioned Jesus's resurrection. At Mary's tomb, he demanded that it be opened so that he could have proof that she really was dead. The other apostles obeyed reluctantly, and when they opened the tomb it was filled to overflowing with lilies and roses – Mary's flowers. Suddenly a lily appeared at Doubting Thomas's feet. When he raised his eyes, he beheld Mary floating above him.

CHAPTER FIVE

DEATH BY VIOLENCE OR MISADVENTURE

There are many plant legends that have themes of death from violent and unnatural causes. Such deaths cause fear, anxiety, and superstition in the living, who worry that the mysterious forces of fate may strike them next. It is an understandable mental step to associate the equally awe-inspiring forces of plant growth, death, and rebirth with our own mortality.

Wood taken from the gallows was used in witchcraft, especially for black magic. In Iceland, it was believed that ash trees appeared and grew on the graves of innocent people who had been put to death unfairly. In Borneo, the souls of the dead were believed to reside in certain trees of the forest.

Similarly, in Korea there were trees associated with the spirits of the dead. It was

51

believed that the spirits of those unfortunate people who died of pestilence or by the side of the road would move to a tree. Certain trees that looked very old and gnarled were assumed to be the homes of spirits of people who died before the age of sixty, possibly because of the malign influence of the tree itself.

In parts of England, Wales, and Scotland, the dwarf elder (*Sambucas ebulus*) was believed to grow only where human blood had been spilled. More specifically, the bitter, bad-smelling plant was associated with an older belief that it grew from the blood of the invading Danes killed in battle; it did indeed grow in great profusion at some of the sites of major skirmishes with the Danes. Two of the dwarf elder's folk names were Danewort (*wort* means plant) and Blood Elder.

In Dante's *Inferno*, one of the circles of hell contains the souls of people who committed suicide. Their punishment for their sin against God is to be entombed within a living oak tree, or transformed into the oak. This macabre forest is infested with predatory harpies who pluck at the oak leaves and the bark until the trees bleed and the tortured souls within cry out in agony.

The famous purple/pink heather, or heath (*Calluna vulgaris*), that covers the hills of Scotland is said to have gotten its name from the fierce fighting between the early Christians and the native Picts. The pagan Picts resisted the armed missionaries' orders that they convert to Christianity. The blood of the vanquished Picts – the heathens – was spilled on the plants of the battlefields. The heather was forever stained, both with blood and a name associating it with savagery.

Jacob Grimm, one of the Brothers Grimm, in his book *Teutonic Mythology* (1882) mentions a motif found in some Old Bohemian folk songs. The songs tell of an oak tree that grows from the grave of a murdered man. On the oak tree are perched sacred sparrowhawks who squawk loudly, broadcasting the news about the murder.

There are several Asian myths about the origin of the coconut. In Sri Lanka, the fruit was said to have sprouted from the head of the buried corpse of a royal astrologer. A Chinese name for coconut was "the head of the Prince of Yue," from the legend that the prince was decapitated by an assassin while drunk. His head was hung on a tree branch and was transformed into a coconut with a pair of eyes in the shell. Among many Pacific peoples, the similarity of the coconut with the human head led to using the fruit in place of a human victim in ritual sacrifice.

Parijat (*Nyctanthes arbor-tristis*), native to India and southern Asia, is also known as night-blooming jasmine, coral jasmine, and the tree of sorrow. A small shrub or tree, Parijat has beautiful, fragrant white flowers that bloom at sunset and die by sunrise. There are several myths about this plant. One sad story tells how Princess Parijataka was in love with the Sun, but he would not have her. The brokenhearted princess committed suicide. The Parijat tree magically sprang up from her ashes. Even now the flowers appear only at night, because the princess and the Sun can never be together. The petals that fall by morning are said to be the tears shed by the princess in her grief.

The blood tree, a tree that provided a strong dark-red dye for Aztec cotton textiles, had a legend. There was a prince who loved to adorn himself with gold and precious gems. To satisfy his lust for jewels, he had a gang of thieves who worked for him. The prince's spies would alert him if a merchant was spotted traveling from town to town, and he would disguise himself and ride ahead with the thieves to ambush and rob the unlucky merchant.

After the prince had paid the gang out of the stolen loot, he dismissed them all except for a slave, and worked with the slave to bury the treasure. But when the slave turned his back on the prince to lower the treasure into the hole, the fiendish prince killed him. The dead slave fell into the pit with the treasure, and the prince covered him with dirt, because in his mind the best guard for a treasure was a ghost, who had all eternity to be vigilant.

The prince repeated his crimes for several years, but eventually he paid the price. After robbing a travelling merchant, he showed a new slave where to dig the hole for the treasure. Suddenly the slave turned and killed him with one blow of the spade. It was the prince's turn to be buried in a rough grave, but this time the treasure left with the slave.

All the places where the prince had dug a pit for a corpse and a treasure began to sprout blood trees. And the tree growing from the robber prince's grave yielded the sap that made the darkest, reddest dye of all.

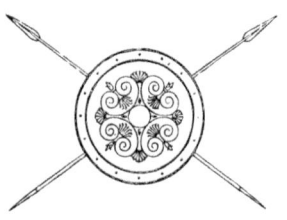

In the *Aeneid* of Virgil, the hero Aeneas journeys to Thrace. Wanting to make a sacrifice to Venus there, he comes to a grove of young trees and tries to pull one up to make an altar. But blood pours out of the tree, and a voice cries out for him to stop. It is the spirit of Polydore (or Polydorus), who had been murdered there by the King of Thrace. The spears that had been used to kill him had become stuck deep in the earth and had grown up through and around his body, so that he was transformed into one of the trees in the gruesome grove. Aeneas and his companions perform a proper funeral ceremony for Polydore in the hope that his spirit can find peace.

The Greek mathematician and philosopher Pythagoras was also famous for his rules for daily living. In addition to requiring vegetarianism, he shunned the eating of beans, because he believed that the souls of some dead humans resided in beans before being reincarnated. He was said to have cited the resemblance between a bean in its early sprouting stages and a human fetus. (The legume to which he referred is likely the fava bean, *Vicia faba*. Similar taboos against eating these beans, and associations of the beans with death, also existed in other cultures, but Pythagoras was the most famous believer.) Some versions of the story of his death describe Pythagoras as being chased by enemies into a bean field. Rather than trample on the bean plants and kill what he believed were fellow humans, he allowed himself to be taken by the murderous mob.

According to folklorist Charles Skinner, there was once a popular variety of American apple called Micah Rood, or Bloody Hearts. They were "sweet of flavor, fragrant, handsomely red outside, and while most of the flesh is white, there is at the core a red spot that represents human blood." A story was traced back to Franklin, Connecticut, where a farmer named Micah Rood lived in the late 1700s. In those times much commerce was done with itinerant peddlers, and these early traveling salesmen sometimes fell victim to violence because of the purses of money they might be carrying.

A peddler who had recently been trading with the local citizens was found dead under an apple tree on Micah Rood's farm, his skull cracked open and his money stolen. Rood was suspected of murder, but there was no proof. He became a recluse to shut out the whisperings of his neighbors.

Later that year, the tree against which the unfortunate victim had bled and died bore red apples instead of its normal yellow. And from then on the tree's fruit had the red mark at the core, like a bloodstain. It was said that every apple was a curse on Micah Rood; he and his farm fell into decay and disrepair, and he died. The tree lived on, and grafts from it spread the apple to orchards across Connecticut and other states. It was once widely cultivated, but I have not been able to find a Micah Rood apple available today. I fear it has been lost like so many other early heirloom varieties.

Luckily a similar heirloom variety of apple, also with a gruesome legend and a sensational appearance, still thrives in the United Kingdom. The Bloody Ploughman apple was first recorded in 1883, in Scotland. Like the Micah Rood apple, it has red "bloodstains" in its flesh, and dark, blood-red skin. The tale behind the name is that a laborer was regularly stealing apples from a Scottish estate, but he got caught and was shot dead. His widow threw the apples out onto the midden with the refuse, thinking them unlucky. A tree sprouted there, grew into a tree, bore new apples, and was given the spooky new name. Bloody Ploughman apples are said to be juicy and crisp, a mid-season variety when grown in southeast England.

CHAPTER SIX

ORIGINS OF STAPLE FOODS

There are many legends from throughout the world that tell of a human origin of important crops and staple foods. These myths often describe the voluntary sacrifice of the crop originator's life, and a transfiguration of a person into a plant.

The Cherokee story of Selu the Corn Mother is one version of the Native American Indian legends that explain how people came to have this staple food crop. As told by Wahnenauhi (Lucy Lowery Hoyt Keys) in the late 1800s, the early Man and Woman (Kanati and Selu) always had plenty of corn and game to feed their large family. With no trouble or effort, every day the father would go out and return shortly with a fresh deer or turkey or other good game. And every day the mother set out with an empty basket but came back quickly with a generous supply of ears of corn, which she would shell and pound into cornmeal for bread.

As the children grew older, they began to wonder where the corn and the game came from. They decided to find the source of their sustenance. The next day some of them followed Kanati when he left on his daily ritual. They saw him go into a cave camouflaged by a large stone. Inside the cave were all the different kinds of animals. Kanati called to one, a deer, and it willingly came to him. He led it out of the cave, covered the opening, and headed toward home with the deer. The children went to move the stone, but as the entrance was revealed, all the animals made a rush at the opening and escaped into the wilderness.

The other children had followed their mother Selu as she left with her empty basket. She went inside a small cabin that they had never seen before. Through a small crack in the cabin the children could watch what she did next. Placing her basket on the ground in front of her, Selu began to dance and jump up and down. As she shook and hopped and stamped, plump ears of corn began to drop into the basket until it was full. Selu took the basket, headed home, and began to prepare the morning meal as usual.

As the family sat down to eat, Kanati told the children that he knew what they had done, and that now he would have to die. Because the children had allowed all the animals to escape from the cave, now they would have to hunt the game in the wilderness to survive. He gave them bows and arrows and told them that they would have to learn how to use them to survive.

Selu told the children that she, too, would have to die because they had discovered her secret. The only thing she could do for them now so that they would not starve was to give them these instructions: When she was dead the children must drag her body over the ground and all around. Wherever her body was dragged, corn would grow from the soil. From that corn they were to make cornmeal for their bread, but they must also remember to always save some of the corn for seed and plant it anew every year.

The breadfruit (*Artocarpus altilis*) grows throughout the Pacific islands. A legend describing the origin of this staple food reveals its importance to the Polynesians:

A long time ago, people ate red earth. There was a husband and wife who had only one child, a son they loved very much. The boy was sickly and could not eat the red earth. The father saw that the boy was wasting away. He told the mother, "I fear our son will die because he can't eat the red earth. He needs food. I will die and change into food for him. I will pray to my god to help me do this."

That evening, he told his wife that his prayer had been answered. "I will die soon. This is what you must do when I am dead: break my body up into pieces and bury them in different places around our yard. Go inside and wait. When you hear a sound like a ripe fruit falling on the ground, it will be me; I will have become food for the boy." The wife followed his instructions, burying the pieces of his body, and waited all night for the sound of the falling fruit. When the sun came up she walked with her son out into the yard, where they saw a beautiful, strong tree. It was covered with ripe breadfruit among its glossy green leaves. The boy and his mother gathered the breadfruit, made some an offering to the god and to the king, and roasted and ate the rest. The boy became healthy and strong.

The Polynesians also had similar traditional tales for the origin of the coconut (grown from a man's head), the chestnut (from human kidneys), yams (from a man's legs), and other food plants.

Manioc (*Manihot esculenta*), also called cassava or yucca, is a shrub native to South America. A starchy flour is made from its root, and it is a staple food of the indigenous peoples of Brazil. A traditional story tells where this important food came from. There was an old man named Mani, the beloved leader of his village. When he knew he was about to die, he promised his people that he would return to help them and provide for them. He instructed them to dig in the ground of his grave, one year after his death. He died, and a year later, the villagers remembered Mani's promise. When they dug up his grave they discovered the first manioc root – Mani's body had been changed into the food that would sustain them into the future.

CHAPTER SEVEN

THE HAUNTED GARDEN IN CONTEMPORARY CULTURE

The theme of transfiguration of humans into plants will probably persist in culture as long as there is culture. Plant/human hybrids and anthropomorphic flowers and trees are found today in all art forms and popular media.

Ovid's *Metamorphoses* remains relevant. It inspired the three Titian paintings at the heart of "Metamorphosis: Titian 2012," a multi-arts exhibition at the National Gallery, London. Artists were commissioned to create new music, dance, film, and visual art for the show. Also based on Ovid is the 1996 play *Metamorphoses* by the American playwright Mary Zimmerman, which was seen on Broadway in 2002.

Popular entertainment often showcases fantasy plant-people in films, animated cartoons, plays, comics, and, of course, in advertising. In *Invasion of the Body*

69

Snatchers, both the 1956 original film and the 1978 sequel, alien plant pods grow into humanoid forms. *Little Shop of Horrors*, both the musical and the movie, features a giant talking, singing, man-eating plant named Audrey II. A more benign example of a plant/person is the jolly Green Giant, the long-standing iconic advertising character for a brand of frozen and canned vegetables.

The Floronic Man (also known as Dr. Jason Woodrue) is a character from DC Comics. Also named the Plant Master and Floro, he is a villain with vast botanical knowledge who creates a formula that turns him into a half-plant, half-human. In "Saga of the Swamp Thing" (Alan Moore, 1984), the Floronic Man attempts to destroy all nonplant life on Earth. (Swamp Thing himself, also a humanoid/plant, has been the subject of films, a live-action TV show, and an animated series.) A related character is Poison Ivy, also a villain in the Batman comics and films. Partly inspired by Nathaniel Hawthorne's short story "Rappaccini's Daughter," Poison Ivy has powers over plants, secretes plant poisons, and is immune to plant toxins. These abilities resulted from her having been subjected to dangerous experiments in which she was injected with deadly botanical concoctions.

The Secret Life of Plants by Peter Tompkins and Christopher Bird, first published in 1973, was a huge bestseller that popularized the idea of plants as sentient beings. Skeptics dismissed the cited research as pseudoscience, but many readers described the book as life-changing. Experiments in psychobotany seemed to reveal that plants were sensitive to human emotion and had telepathic ability, among other powers. According to the authors, "Evidence now supports the vision of the poet and the philosopher that plants are living, breathing, communicating creatures, endowed with personality and the attributes of the soul."

Such a view is largely in accord with the beliefs of many of the Neo-Pagan religions, which are finding increased acceptance. A sense of oneness with Nature and the interconnectedness of everything, and a conviction that Nature is holy and divine, is reflected in much Neo-Pagan thought. Plant/human hybrids appear in the imagery of these religions, such as the Green Man and vegetation deities and spirits.

The concept of humans being changed into plants has acquired a new twist with the alarming rise of genetically modified organisms (GMOs) in corporate agriculture. In the United States, as much as 80 percent of the acreage devoted to major crops such as soybeans and corn is being planted with GMO-altered seeds. GMOs are created by using genetic engineering and biotechnology to change the DNA of an organism.

Sometimes genetic material from animals or insects is introduced into the DNA of a plant in an effort to create various new properties such as disease resistance or delayed spoiling. While that may seem innocuous, the long-term effects of human consumption of foods containing GMOs have not been sufficiently studied. Many people fear that GMOs may damage human health and endanger fragile ecosystems. It is not such a great leap to go from these fears to considering the possibility that the Frankenstein-like manipulation of genes in our food supply could lead to strange vegetable-human mutations.

One of the stranger and more infamous "science news" stories that made the rounds of the Internet was a report that an 18-year-old Armenian girl was mutating into a cactus. According to a 2005 Pravda report endlessly circulated online, the girl complained of a painful abscess on her wrist. When doctors took off her bandage, they found thorns protruding from her hand. The thorns were removed but new ones grew. Tests confirmed that these were thorns of a common cactus plant. The girl had pricked herself on a cactus while tending her indoor potted plants, and it was believed that plant cells had become parasites in her system. Even after the entire abscess was surgically removed, more thorns grew in new places, and the girl was told nothing more could be done to help her.

I have been unable to verify the truth or untruth of this report, so I assume it is an urban legend or has a more conventional scientific explanation. Nevertheless, the story lives on through a kind of bardic tradition of the Web.

In the Digital Age, it is somewhat comforting that there are new "myths" arising that almost equal Ovid's classical tales in their sensationalism. New stories continue to arise, joining the ancient legends. All of them can be heard in the whispers of the flowers, trees, and plants of the Haunted Garden.

SELECTED BIBLIOGRAPHY

Bennett, Jennifer. *Lilies of the Hearth: The Historical Relationship Between Women and Plants.* Camden East, Ontario: Camden House, 1993.

Cohen, Norm. *Folk Music: A Regional Exploration.* Westport, CT: Greenwood Press, 2005.

Flanner, Hildegarde. *At the Gentle Mercy of Plants: Essays and Poems.* Santa Barbara, CA: John Daniel, 1986.

Gordon, Lesley. *The Mystery and Magic of Trees and Flowers.* London: Grange Books, 1993.

Grieve, Mrs. M. *A Modern Herbal (Volume I).* Originally published 1931. Mineola, NY: Dover Publications, 1971.

Heath, Jennifer. *The Echoing Green: The Garden in Myth and Memory.* New York: Plume, 2000.

Mooney, James. *History, Myths, and Sacred Formulas of the Cherokees.* Originally published in 2 volumes in 1891 and 1900.

Ovid. *The Metamorphoses.* Translated by Horace Gregory. New York: Mentor, 1960.

Paterson, Jacqueline Memory. *Tree Wisdom: The Definitive Guidebook to the Myth, Folklore, and Healing Power of Trees.* London: Thorsons, 1996.

Porteous, Alexander. *The Forest in Folklore and Mythology*. Mineola, NY: Dover, 2002 [originally published 1928 by Macmillan, NY].

Pravda.ru [online; no author stated]. "Terrible mutations may turn humans into plants or animals." http://english.pravda.ru/health/20-12-2005/9418-mutation-0/ . Dec. 20, 2005.

Ricciuti, Edward R. *The Devil's Garden: Facts and Folklore of Perilous Plants*. New York: Walker, 1978.

Skinner, Charles M. *Myths and Legends of Flowers, Trees, Fruits, and Plants in All Ages and in All Climes*. Amsterdam: Fredonia Books, 2002 [reprinted from the 1911 edition].

Tompkins, Peter and Bird, Christopher. *The Secret Life of Plants*. New York: Avon Books, 1974.

Walker, Barbara G. *The Woman's Encyclopedia of Myths and Secrets*. New York: Harper & Row, 1983.

Williams, Ellis. *Polynesian Researches, 2nd ed.*, 1832.

Yang, Lihui, *et al. Handbook of Chinese Mythology*. New York: Oxford University Press, 2005.

Printed in Great Britain
by Amazon